IKEBANA

SOGETSU FLOWER ARRANGEMENT
FOR BEGINNERS

by SOFU TESHIGAHARA

in New York

"IKEBANA", JAPANESE FLOWER ARRANGEMENT

Man's use of flowers as a means of decoration would seem to be as old as the recorded history of civilization.

Excavations, particularly in the East, have given evidence of early use of flowers for personal and household adornment as well as in various acts of worship. The origin of Ikebana may be said to reach back as far as seven hundred years. It continues to flourish and develop

IKEBANA INTERNATIONAL

Washington D.C. Chapter
March 29-30-31—1962
Marriott Motel
Twin Bridges

today with many books and magazines published to promote its practice. It is taught in Japanese high schools as a form of art together with calligraphy and painting. There are approximately sixty well organized schools of Ikebana. among which the Ikenobo, Ohara and Sogetsu are generally accepted as the most important. The deans of these three schools are the honorary flower master advisors to Ikebana International.

The first Ikebana styles were products of Buddhist thought and its practitioners were priests. In about the 13th century, Ikebana entered the home of the samurai warriors. The "Tokonoma" designated as the most sacred place in the home was added to the architecture of the room and was inevitably the setting for a flower arrangement. With their place determined, the flower arrangements of the time became very similar, differing only with the flowers used. These arrangements soon developed mannerisms and ceased to be creative. In 1868 the Meiji Restoration brought industrialization to the country but many traditional customs were carried over from the feudal system including Ikebana in a degenerated form.

SOON HOWEVER, A NEW MOVEMENT IN IKEBANA WAS CREATED.

An Ikebana instructor, Hisatsugu Teshigahara founded his "Japan Floral Institute" and introduced modern methods that seemed rather progressive at the time. Hisatsugu had a son, Sofu, who is the founder and dean of the Sogetsu School and the undisputed master of Ikebana in Japan at present.

Sofu Teshigahara was born in Tokyo, Japan, in 1900. From the age of seven he was taught the art of Ikebana by his father. After graduating from school he taught Ikebana under his father until he reached the age of 25 when his independent spirit demanded a freer expression. In May, 1926 he founded his school, which he named the "Sogetsu School". In its organization the Sogetsu School was not wholly new; the predominating influences of the Sogetsu School stemmed from Sofu's individual genius and determination in elevating the art of Ikebana from an attractive craft to a form of art. Doing away with all fixed methods, Sofu has given fresh consideration to each arrangement in terms of the materials at hand with his own will and feeling at the time. This new philosophical approach echoed throughout Japan. He has today almost a million students and followers in Japan and many overseas.

The most significant characteristic of the Sogetsu School is its ideal adaptability. In other words, it aims at making arrangements that will suit any surrounding, Western or Japanese, with unlimited kinds of flowers or tree branches, and, for which any kind of vessel, not necessarily made for the purpose, may be used. For instance, a successful arrangement may, in this new style, be made in a jug or new wash-basin, as beautifully as in a proper vase. Moreover, the form is not meant to be invariable but to be developed into forms which will harmonize with new environments which may be evolved in the future.

Sofu's most talented disciple is his daughter, Kasumi, the natural successor to the Sogetsu School. Her graceful personality and natural ability will be perceived through her Ikebana.

Sofu is also a sculptor of great originality and his work has been exhibited at the Galerie Stadler in Paris and the Martha Jackson Gallery in New York. In the course of events, he has been decorated by the French Government with the "Ordre des Arts et des Lettres" and the "Legion d'honneur" in 1961 and received the "Laurel of the International Center of Aesthetic Research" in Turin, Italy, in 1960. In April 1962 he was awarded the Education Minister's Prize by the Japanese Government for his contributions to the Art Encouragement Program.

The Sogetsu School is now active in training and instructing students in the art of Ikebana both at home and abroad and publishing books and periodicals in English and Japanese.

in London

in Paris

FUNDAMENTAL "MORIBANA" AND "NAGEIRE" STYLES

The fundamental styles known as "Moribana", shallow container arrangements, and "Nageire", vase arrangements, are introduced to assist those who are attempting Japanese flower arrangements for the first time.

As in the case of music or painting, style in flower arrangement can be accomplished only by earnest study. The secret of learning to arrange flowers artistically is found in the earnest study of the fundamental styles.

EQUIPMENT REQUIRED

Fig. 1 Types of containers that are suitable for "Moribana" arrangements.

Fig. 2 Types of vases used for "Nageire" arrangements.

Fig. 3 Contemporary containers which can be used effectively for both the "Moribana" and "Nageire" self-expression styles.

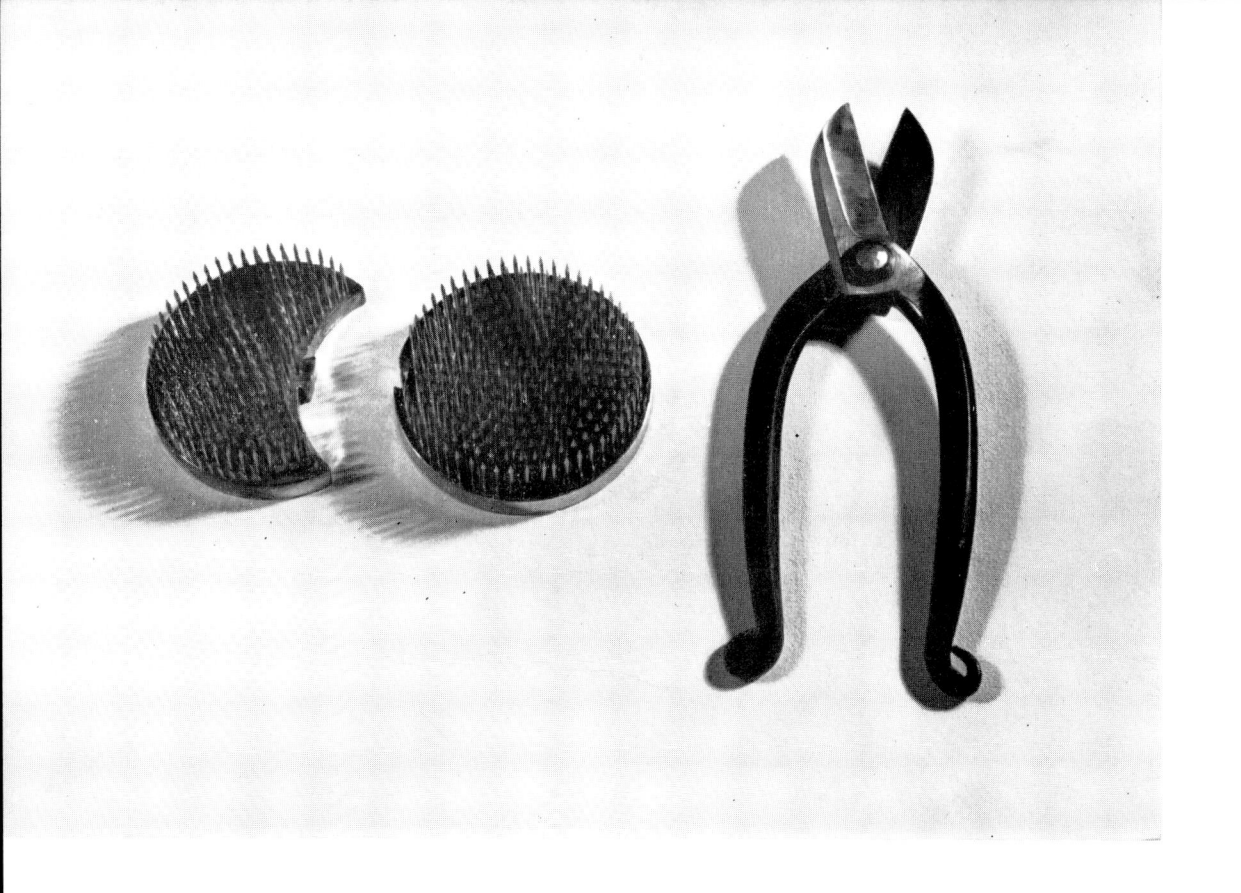

Fig. 4 A pair of scissors and "Kenzan" or needle point holders are needed. It is recommended that the flower arrangement students obtain several sizes of holders, both small and large.

Suggested Materials for Beginners

The ideal basic materials are branches or shrubs that are comparatively straight and not too brittle.

If leafy branches are used together with flowers, the holder can be well concealed by cutting the branches short and inserting them around the holder.

Good branch materials—bridal wreath, pussy willow, water willow, wood berries, hydrangea, and witch hazel.

Flowers—mustard flower, marigold, daisy, chrysanthemum, peony, lily and stock.

After experiments with these suggested materials, skill will be developed so that the arranger will be able to use his discretion in selecting branches and flowers.

Material :—Chrysanthemum

Container :—Lacquer dish

Style :—Basic upright style

Materials :—
  Bitter-sweet,
  Lily and Fern
Container :—
  Ceramic vase
Style :—
  Basic slanting arrangement

Materials :—
  Acacia and
  Chrysanthemum
Container :—
  Ceramic basin
Style :—
  Basic slanting arrangement

TECHNIQUES

Cutting:

It is important to cut the branches or stems correctly. Branches should be cut at an angle, and flower stems should be cut across horizontally at the stem end. When cutting thick branches, they should be cut again at a sharper angle to make a sharper point at the base.

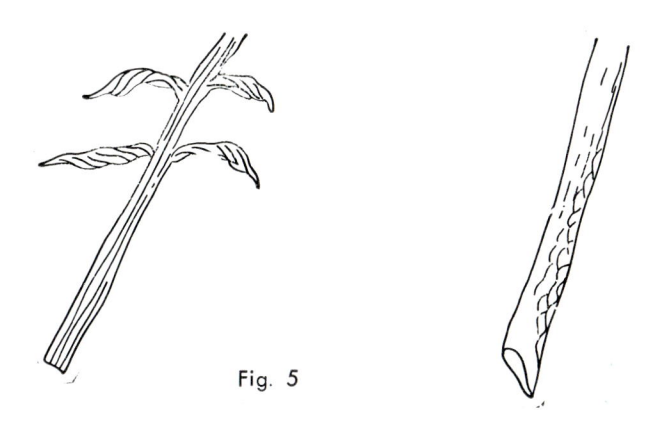

Fig. 5

Trimming:

In a Japanese flower arrangement the branches or flowers are carefully trimmed. All bruised or torn flowers or leaves must be removed or trimmed. Branches that cross each other should be removed or bent away from other branches.

The beginner is often afraid to trim branches but with constant practice the eye will become accustomed to the correct lines.

Bending:

Branches—It is seldom that a branch is naturally graceful. Most branches seen in a Japanese arrangement are skillfully bent to give the appearance of growing gracefully out of the water. Fig. 6 shows the correct way to bend a branch. Fig. 7 shows the wrong technique in attempting to bend a branch.

Fig. 6

Fig. 7

The most important thing to remember is to be sure to hold the branch with both hands close together, as illustrated. In bending, do not attempt to bend the branch with force and in one concentrated area. Several curves are often necessary to achieve a graceful line.

Flowers—Flowers are more apt to snap when bending than branches. Care should be taken to twist and bend the stem simultaneously. This will prevent the stem from breaking.

Fig. 8

Technique of Inserting Plant Materials in a Needle Point Holder

The needle point holder known as "kenzan" in Japanese is recommended to support the plant materials used. After the plant material has been cut at a slant, first insert it upright in the holder and then tilt it in any desirable direction, with the cut edge pointing upward.

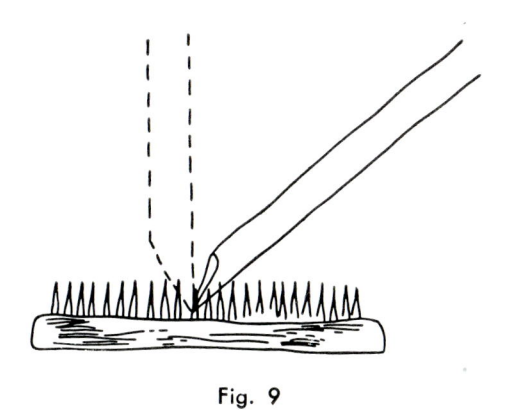

Fig. 9

When a branch or flower is too thin to be inserted in the holder, cut a short thick stem from a flower and insert the slender stem inside it, as illustrated. Other recommended methods are to wrap tissue paper around the slender stem, or tie another piece of twig to the slender stem, as illustrated.

Fig. 10    Fig. 11

Technique of Inserting Plant Materials in a Vase

Vase arrangements are more difficult to do than the low bowl type. There are two ways to secure branches in a vase. A cylindrical vase is the easiest type to use for tall arrangements. Figures 12—15 illustrate the methods used.

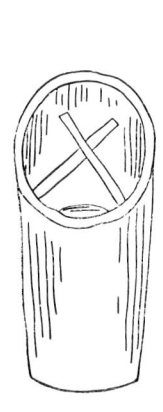

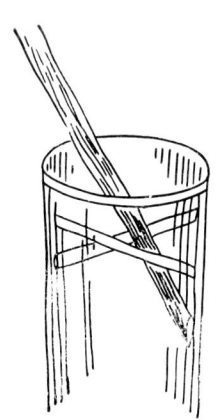

Fig. 12

Cross-bar Fixture:

This type of fixture is made by crossing two small twigs about one half inch down from the mouth of the vase. Insert the branch into the vase with the cross-bar fixture already secured together. The ends of the branches are cut at an angle; this will enable the ends of the branches to rest securely against the walls of the vase. This cross-bar fixture should be used in cylindrical vases only.

Single Bar Fixture:

This type of fixture will secure ill-proportioned branches. Split the base of the branch and place a twig, measuring a little longer than the diameter of the vase, in the split branch. Then tie with wet rice straw or florist wire. Make sure that the ends of the twig are firmly

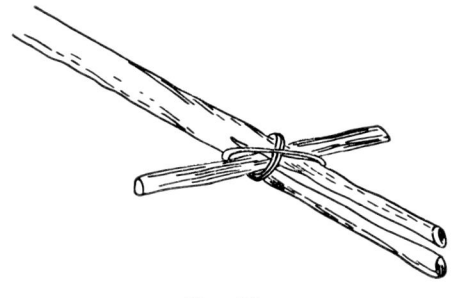

Fig. 13

touching the inside walls of the vase at its diameter. The branch ends should be cut at a slant in order to secure a firmer balance.

Vertical Type Fixture:

The vertical type of fixture is excellent for branches that are to be arranged in an upright manner. This type of fixture can be applied to any shape of container.

Take a discarded branch which is fairly thick and cut it a little shorter than the height of the vase. Split the heavier end about three inches. Then hold the branch to be used for the arrangement up to the vase to judge the desirable angle for the composition. When the position of the branch has been decided, split the base and insert in the fixture, as illustrated in the diagram. The split ends should interlock securely.

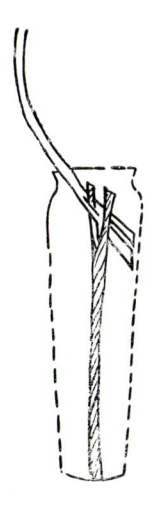

Fig. 14

If the branches used are thin, tie the split ends with wet rice straw or wire.

If the base of the branch fixture rests on the bottom of the vase, and the split ends of the branch used in the arrangement touch the inside wall of the vase, the balance of the material used, regardless of type, will be more secure.

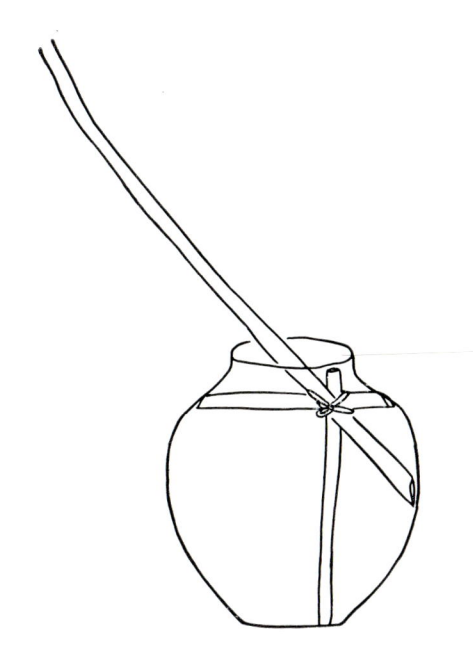

Fixtures for Jar-shaped Vase:

Jar-shaped containers need a special fixture to secure the branches. Neither the cross-bar nor the single bar fixtures can be applied to this type of vase. The branch fixtures should be of two types:

a/ vertical branch measuring almost the height of the vase.

b/ horizontal branch slightly longer than the diameter of the vase at its mouth.

— 15 —

Tie the two branches together as illustrated. It is important to remember that the vertical branch must rest securely on the bottom of the vase and the horizontal branch must press tightly against the walls of the vase.

If the mouth of the container is wide enough, a needle point holder can be used effectively.

INTRODUCTION OF SHIN, SOE & HIKAE

There are three main lines called:
        Longest line--SHIN --(first main branch or stem)
        Medium line--SOE --(second main branch or stem)
        Shortest line--HIKAE--(third main branch or stem)

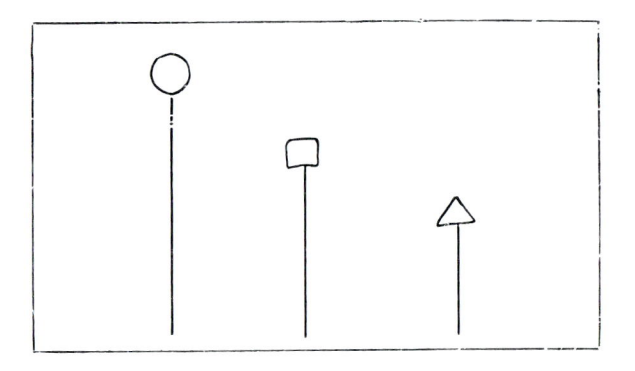

JUSHI (subordinate or additional stems)
    To each line of Shin, Soe and Hikae there may be added supplementary branches or stems. These supplementary lines are called JUSHI, and are cut shorter than their main lines, and any number can be added freely to complete the arrangement.

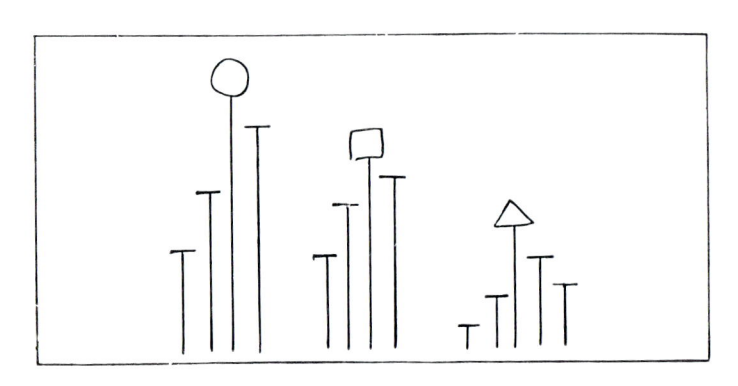

Length of SHIN : —

When the container and the flowers are ready, the next thing to think about is what length to cut the stems.

The beauty of arranged flowers stems from the harmony between flower and container. The Sogetsu School has found that the simplest way of obtaining this harmony is to calculate the length of the Shin according to the size of the container.

The size of the container is determined by adding the depth of a container to its diameter.

In case of an oblong dish, the measurement of the longer side, added to the depth is used as the size of the container.

This same calculation is used for a shallow dish (Moribana) or for a tall vase (Nageire).

"Shin" (The first main stem)········The standard length for the Shin stem is one and one-half times the measurement of the dish or vase. (See the center diagram)

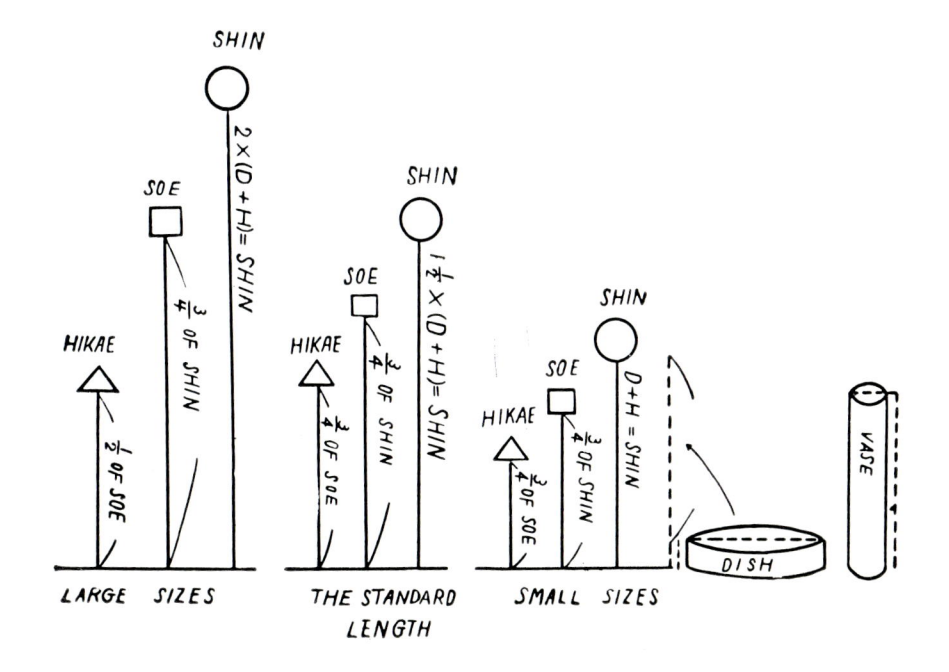

LARGE SIZES | THE STANDARD LENGTH | SMALL SIZES

— 17 —

If a large arrangement is desired, the Shin should be twice the measurement of the vase. If a smaller arrangement is desired, the length should be the same as the measurement of the container.

"Soe" (The second main stem)······Three-fourths the length of Shin.
"Hikae" (The third main stem)······Three-fourths the length of Soe.
"Jushi" (Subordinate stem)······The length should be shorter than the main stems, with no limit to the number used.

It is well to remember these lengths; the fundamental measurements as stated above are those used for all the forms of the Sogetsu School arrangements throughout the country; and it is best to keep this in mind when looking at the photographs of Sogetsu arrangements, so as to visualize the harmony between the flowers and the container.

Although the diameter of the mouth of a tall vase for Nageire is much smaller than that of a shallow dish, as its height can be taken into account when measuring the depth, the same method of calculation may be applied as for shallow dishes.

Moribana and Nageire:—

Moribana includes all types of arrangements in shallow dishes using a kenzan to hold the flowers, and Nageire embraces all arrangements in tall vases not using kenzan.

Moribana is taught first in flower arrangement lessons, as it is easier for inexperienced beginners to imitate this style.

TWO BASIC FORMS

The Sogetsu School has two basic forms which are always taught to beginners.

They are:—
    1. The basic upright arrangement
    2. The basic slanting arrangement

The Upright arrangement has, as the name indicates, the longest Shin standing upright, and even with the other stems slanting the form will still have the accent on its upright position. On the other hand, in the Slanting arrangement the Shin is tilted and even with the other stems in upright positions, the whole will have a slanting effect.

These two basic forms apply to both Moribana and Nageire; so it can be said that the fundamental forms are the same for both the Moribana and Nageire styles.

The basic points are:—
- Easy to arrange
- Any material can be used
- Variable in usage

Basic upright arrangement, Moribana

Materials:—Black-eyed willow and white chrysanthemum.
Container:—Round shallow porcelain dish.

There are very few flowers that can be used just as they come from the florist; usually there are some broken twigs and leaves which must be trimmed off and cleaned. The unnecessary branches must be trimmed off and the leaves, thinned out, if too crowded, to allow the best points of the main branch to stand out. This sounds an easy task. but it is quite difficult at first. It is advisable to conduct some drastic experiments at first without regard for the consequences in order to acquire valuable skill and knowledge.

Preparing flowers for arrangement

The photograph below shows the flowers ready for arrangement. The longest stem of the black-eyed willow on the extreme right is the Shin, and the next one is the Soe and the two stems on the third kenzan from the right are the small stems cut off from the Shin and Soe stems to be used as Jushi. The fourth kenzan from the right holds the chrysanthemum to be used for the Hikae, and the following two flowers on the left are the Jushi for the Hikae.

When using slender or fine material without much body, it would be well to arrange them as the long piece, or the Shin of a large arrangement. Therefore, the length of this black-eyed willow for the Shin is cut twice the length of the dish measurement (the measurement being the depth of the dish added to the diameter).

The Soe is three-fourths of the Shin, and the Hikae is one-half of the Soe. Normally, the Hikae is three-fourths of the Soe, but, when the Shin is cut in double length, it will be too long to have the length of the Hikae three-fourths the length of the Soe. It is more important however to decide the length of the flowers by eye-measure than to adhere too closely to the rule, for even though the flower is cut in the correct length depending on the color of the flower, it sometimes may look longer by optical illusion.

There are no particular set measurements for Jushi, and they can be of any length: but Jushi should not be longer than each of the main stems to which Jushi is added, and also each one of these Jushi should be of a different length.

Correct positions of kenzan

Where to place flowers in the dish:——
The next step is to decide where to place the kenzan in arranging flowers in a shallow dish.

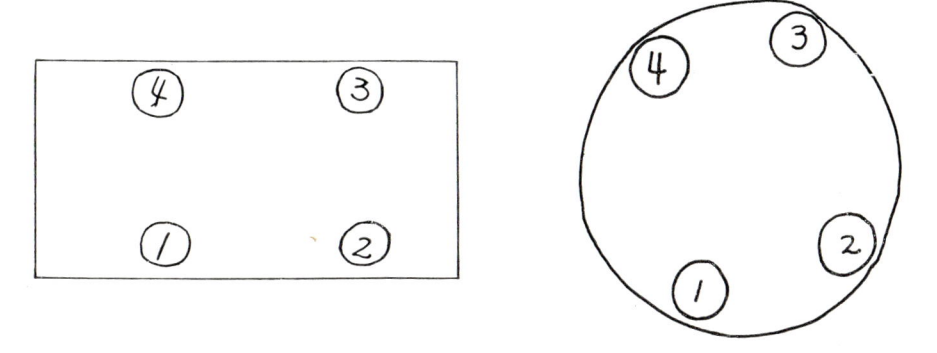

Basically, the kenzan is placed in one or the other of four corners of a dish, as shown in the diagram. This diagram shows only the square and the round dish with the four corners marked. Occasionally the kenzan is placed in spaces other than these corners, but never in the center for a fundamental arrangement.

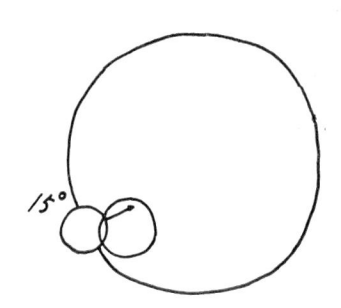

Steps in arrangement

(1) Hold the Shin branch sideways with the front of the leaves of the branch (the side which faces the sunlight) toward you and cut off the end diagonally. Then press down Shin into the center rear of the kenzan, and tilt it 10°—15° forward to left front, diagonally. Of course, the degree of this tilting depends largely on the shape and the type of materials used. (See picture and diagram)

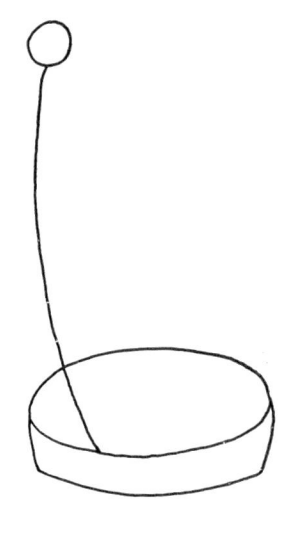

(2) The Soe must go into the left front of the kenzan, and slant diagonally toward the left front at about 40°—50°. (45° here)

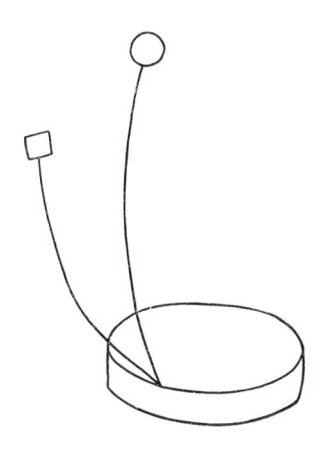

— 23 —

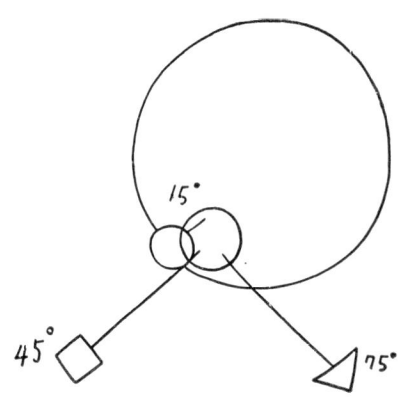

(3) The Hikae, the third main stem, is put in the right front part of the kenzan and tilted 75° diagonally toward the right front.

The stalk of the chrysanthemum used for this Hikae is cut straight across at the end. The stem should be cut under the surface of water, as the plants belonging to the grass family take up water best when cut under water.

Now the three main stems are set; ── as shown in the diagrams at the right.

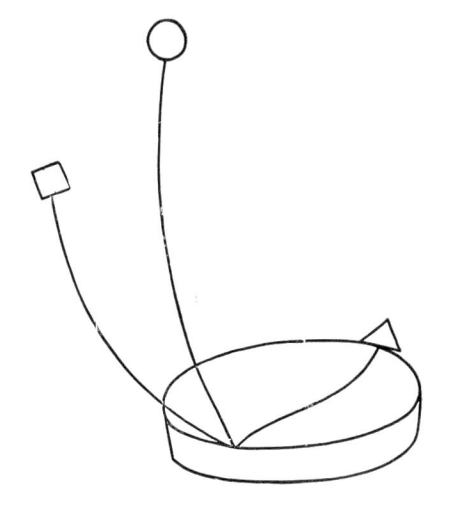

— 24 —

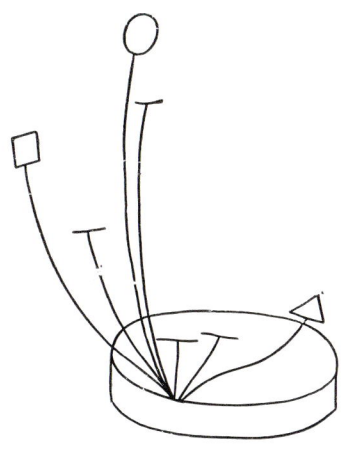

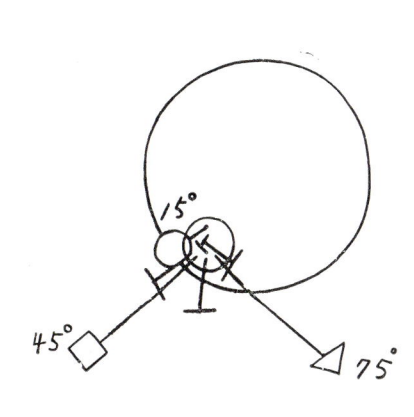

(4) Next, place one Jushi in front of the Shin, and another in between the Shin and Soe.

Take two stalks of chrysanthemum as Jushi for the Hikae, and slant one of them very low and forward to hide the kenzan; and place the trimmed-off leaves with stems around the kenzan until it is completely covered and a finished look is achieved.

Degree of slant of the three main branches

The idea of tilting by degree is rather obscure for beginners, but it will become familiar if the vertical line is considered for the sake of convenience as 0° and the horizontal line as 90°.

The shape of a flower arrangement is composed of height, width and depth: as illustrated in the bird's eye-view diagrams in the preceding pages, they are all tilted forward either to the right or to the left.

Study the diagram showing the degree of slant of the three main stems.

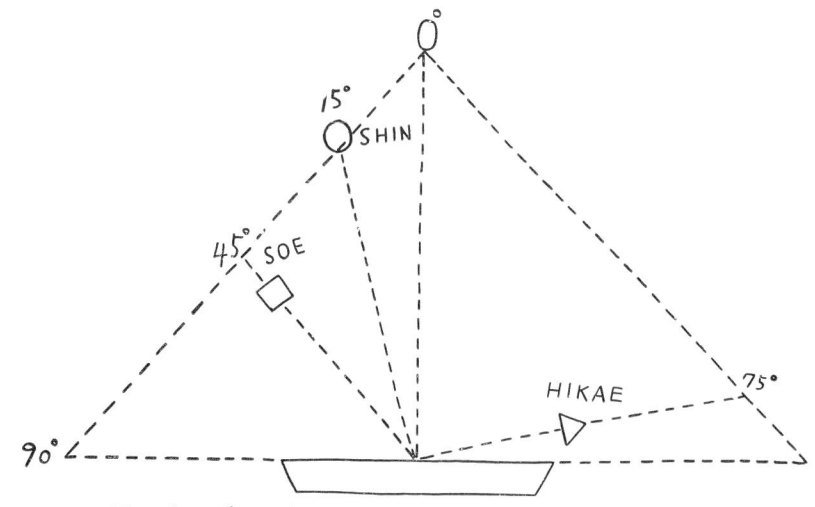

Basic slanting arrangement Moribana

Materials:—— Forsythia and calendula
Cantainer:—— Shallow blue dish

The slanting arrangement Shin will come easily to a person who has practiced the upright arrangement well, and has the knowledge of cutting and fixing, and of the angle of slant.

The upright arrangement Shin has the look of standing upright. When the Shin is tilted to 45°—50°, it is called the slanting arrargement.

The slanting arrangement can be made with these easy-to-arrange materials—forsythia and calendula, with the kenzan placed in the right rear of the dish.

Steps in arrangement

Study the length of the branches shown in the following picture, and reflect on their length in relation to the dish measurement.

Press down the Shin into the left corner of the kenzan and slant it diagonally toward the left front at about 45°. Then place the Soe in the center rear of the kenzan and slant it in the same direction as the Shin; the Soe should, however, be tilted about 15° diagonally to the left front. As shown in the picture and diagrams, the positions of the Shin and Soe in the slanting arrangement are the exact opposite to those in the upright arrangement (note the positions of the branches in the kenzan).

The position of the Hikae is the same as in the upright arrangement, and the photograph shows a 75° tilt diagonally toward the right front. Place two Jushi stems between the Shin and Soe.

The arrangement is finished with one Jushi in front and another at the side of Hikae and the kenzan covered with the trimmed-off leaves as in the upright arrangement. Care should be taken not to allow any leaves to be left immersed in the water as they will suggest untidiness.

Example :—
  Basic upright arrangement

Material :—
  Strelitzia (bird of paradise)

Container :—
  Round porcelain dish

Example :—
  Basic slanting arrangement

Materials :—
  Anthurium and stock

Container :—
  Round porcelain dish

Materials :—
 Phoenix and carnation

Container :—
 Ceramic basin

Style :—
 Basic slanting arrangement

Materials :— Phormium tenax and chrysanthemum

Container :— Lacquer dish

Style :— Basic upright arrangement

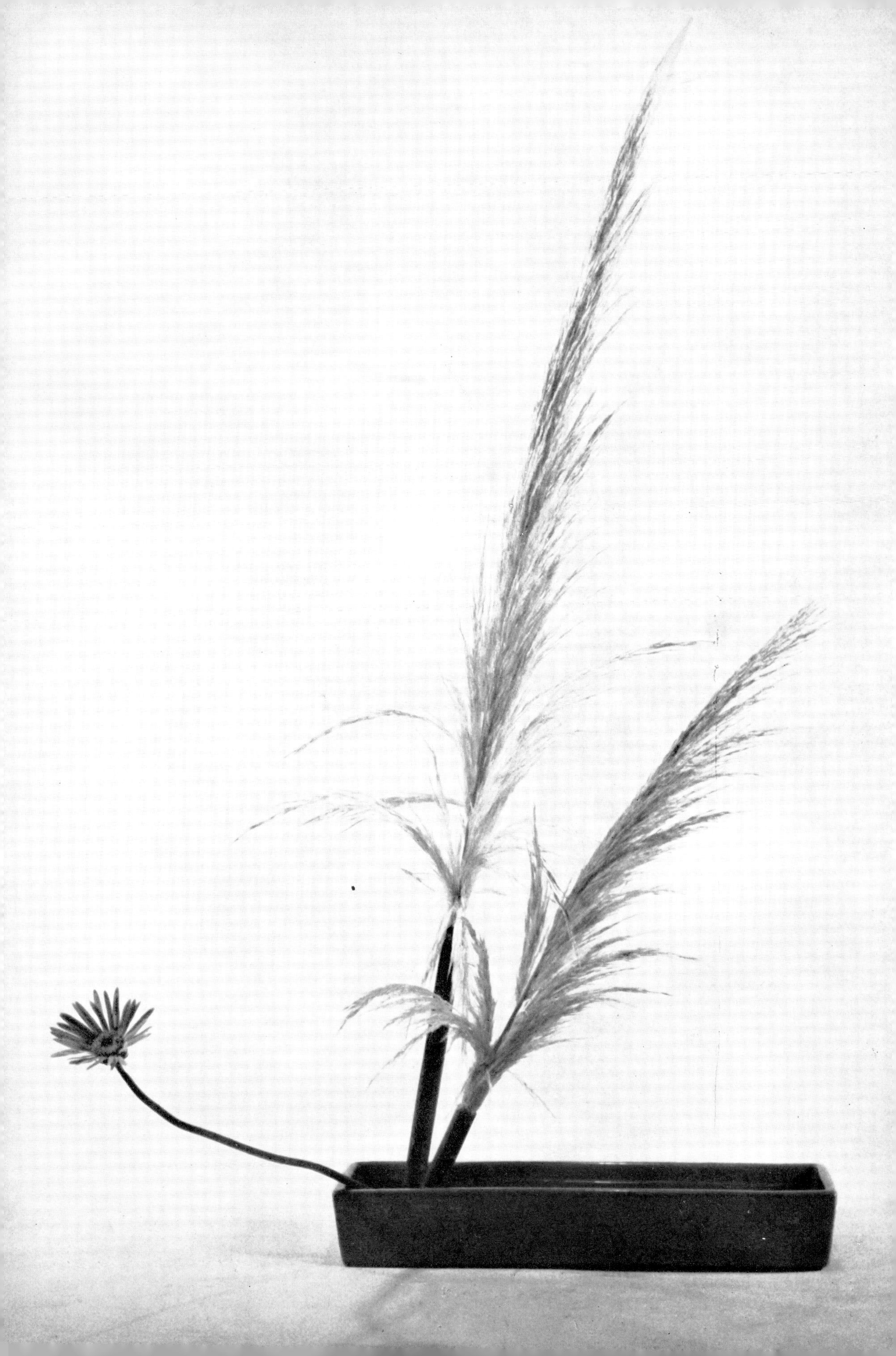

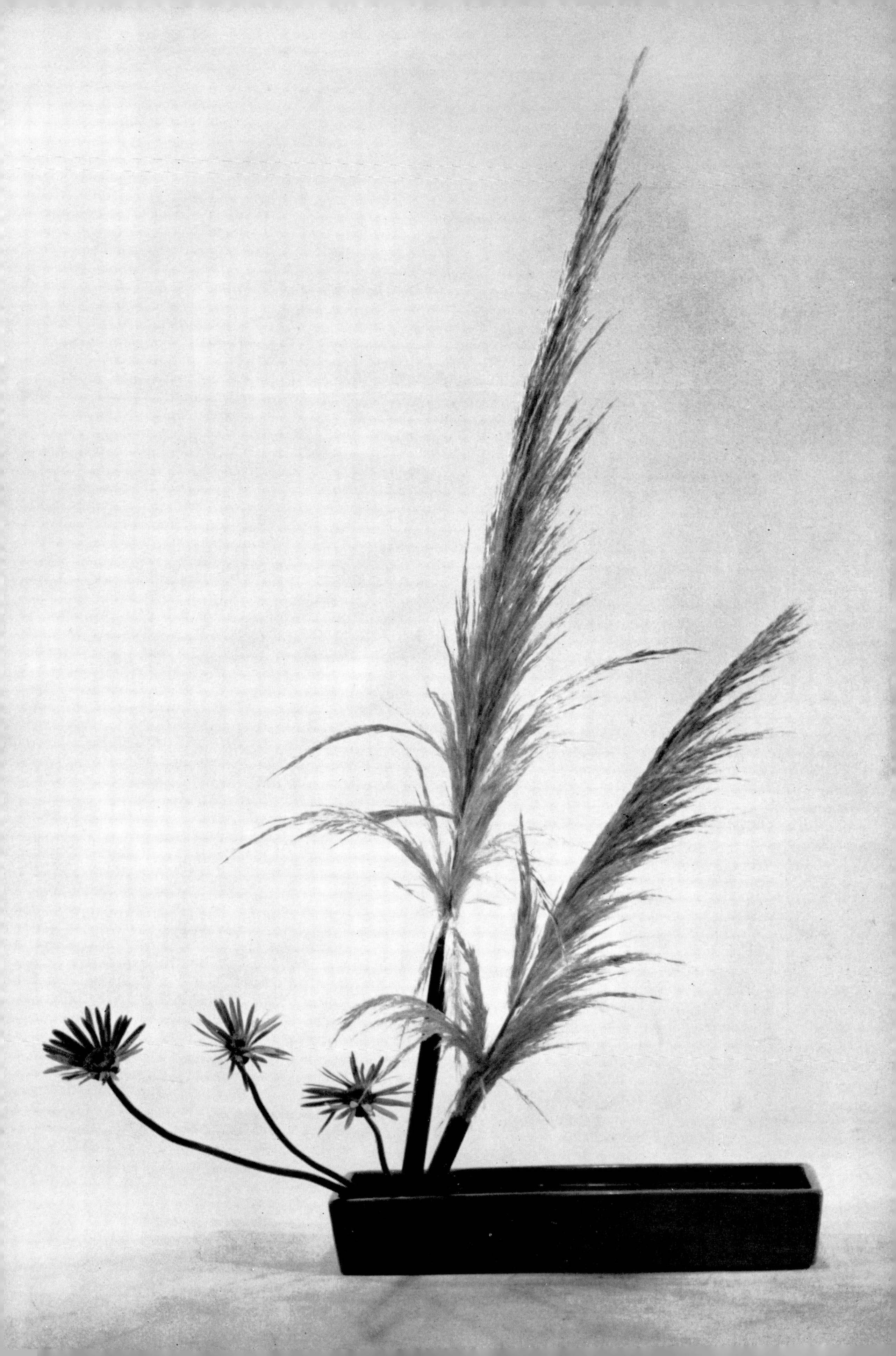

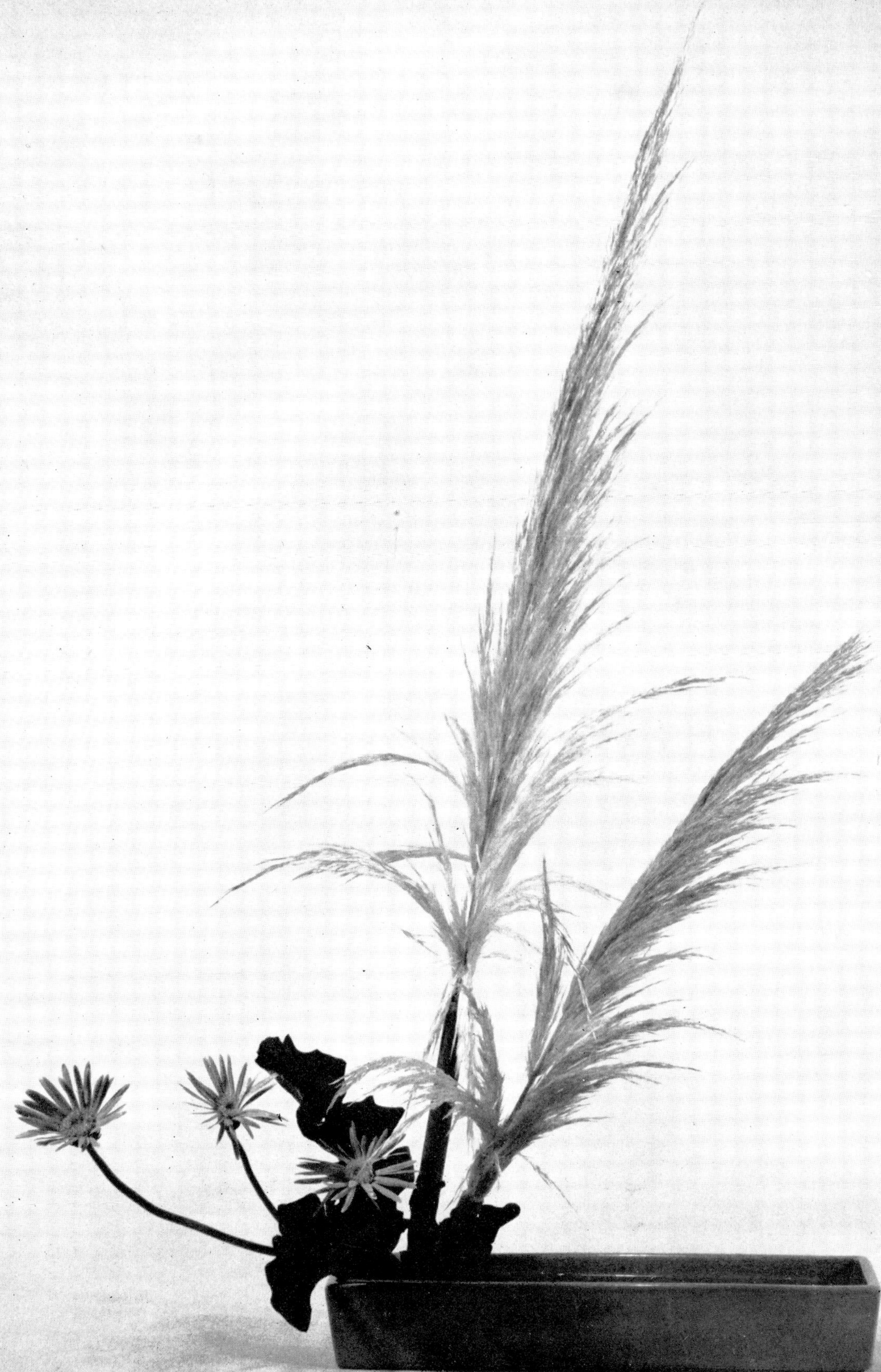

◄

Materials:—
 Pampus grass and Gerbera

Container:—
 Black porcelain dish

Style:—
 Basic upright style

Materials:—
 Quince and Iris

Container:—
 Ceramic vase

Style:—
 Basic upright style

Materials :—Orange branch and Rose
Container :—Ceramic vase
Style :—Basic slanting arrangement

Importance of practice:—

With the Sogetsu School method, a person can learn to arrange not only in the fundamental style, but in any form, using different kinds of materials. Practice with as many different materials as possible is recommended as the best way to achieve proficiency. By changing materials, the same form of arrangement can present a surprisingly varied look.

As in these examples, the plain straight stems are the easiest to use for practice. The combination of tree branches and flowers is commonly used and is also the safest; but flowers alone can be used for arrangements.

Caution must be taken to hide the kenzan, for the kenzan is used for holding the flowers, and is not at all pretty to look at.

Basic upright arrangement, Nageire

Materials :—Wood-berries and yellow chrysanthemums—medium size
Vase : —Tall green porcelain vase

Now that the two basic arrangements in Moribana have been learned, the next step is the upright arrangement of Nageire, with the easy materials of wood-berries and chrysanthemums.

A Moribana arrangement with a kenzan to hold and tilt flowers at any angle is comparatively easy for beginners; but to compose an upright arrangement of Nageire with a slightly curved branch in a tall vase as in the photograph, is a little harder for the beginner.

The picture shows the Shin well fastened in a vase with a vertical type fixture, at a 15° slant same as in Moribana.

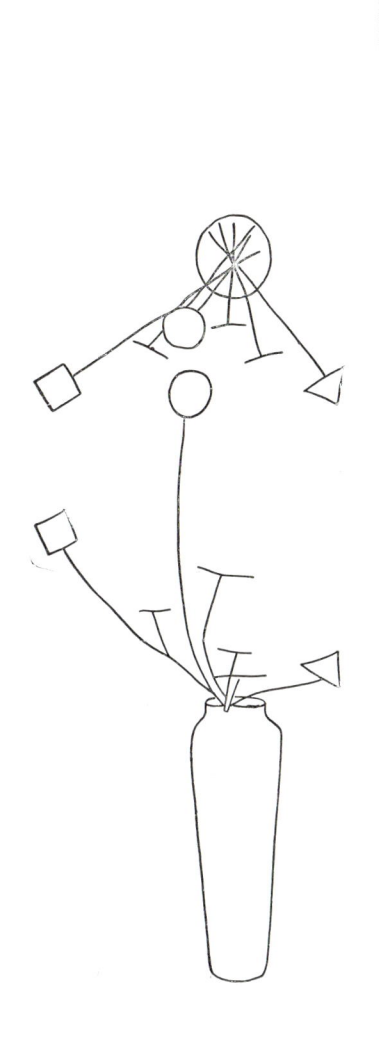

Split the end of the Soe branch, clasp it on to the Shin branch to make it stay firm in its position, and give it a 45° slant as in Moribana.

The picture shows a chrysanthemum Hikae in its place at a 75° slant.

This upright arrangement of Nageire is finished with two Jushi chrysanthemums, one in front and another in back, as shown in the picture.

Basic slanting arrangement, Nageire

Materials: — Mimosa-acacia and lupine
Vase: — Tall brown ceramic vase

    The mimosa-acacia in the picture may look as though it had been left as it came from the florist's, but a number of flowers were removed from the over-crowded clusters, and the leaves were trimmed off considerably in order to give a look of clean simplicity at the mouth of the vase. The thick part of the lupine leaves was also removed to free it from an over-burdened look.

    For this type of vase, with a straight cylindrical shape from the mouth down almost to the bottom, the branches will stay in place, with either the vertical type attachment or the cross-bar fixture.

    The cross-bar fixture is set about one-half inch down from the mouth of the vase as shown in the diagram. The position and the angle of the flowers are about the same as in Moribana, but depending on the shape of the branches it need not be so strict as with Moribana.

    As can be seen in the picture of the completed arrangement, the Shin is tilted 45° to the left front diagonally, while the Soe stands in the back of it at a 15° slant, and the Hikae at a 75° angle is placed diagonally toward the right front. As is shown by the cross-bar fixture diagram, the branches are inserted in the front and the rear sections of the fixture.

    It is very difficult to arrange Nageire in a tall vase when the branches curve in opposite directions at the base. But with patient and gentle bending they can be corrected to the desired shapes.

    Rather than to force one's ability by attempting advanced styles, it is better to study the fundamental forms with thoroughness and patience.

— 39 —

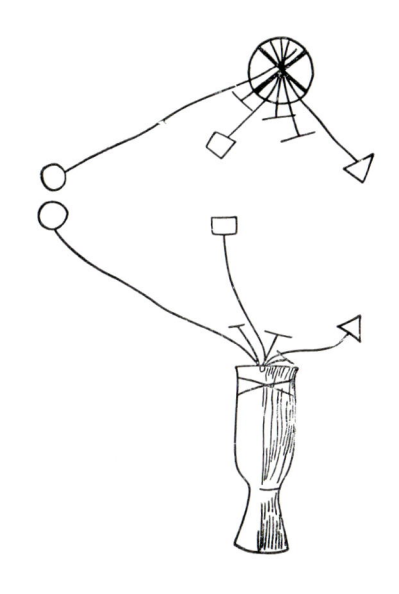

Materials: —Pampas-leaves and dahlia
Container: —Bamboo basket
Style: —Basic upright arrangement

Materials :—Chestnut branches and chrysanthemum
Container:—Ceramic vase
Style : —Basic slanting arrangement

Practice of Variations in Style

To create freely in order to bring out the art in flower arrangement is a very important ideal to strive for; but to achieve this, much practice in basic styles is necessary to prevent doing it at random and becoming conceited.

For those who have mastered the basic styles, there are the variations in style for further study. These styles are not difficult for those who thoroughly understand the arrangement of the basic styles and they will be able to do creative work while continuing to practice these variations of the basic style.

Variation No. 1 upright arrangement

Materials :—Cherry and mustard-flower

Container :—Square yellow ceramic dish

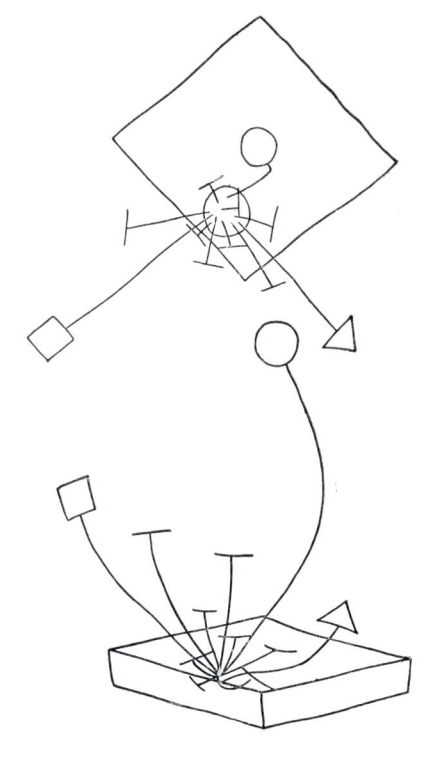

The Shin standing upright in the photograph reveals that this is an upright arrangement.

Pay close attention to the photograph and the diagram, and compare it with the basic upright arrangement. The positions of Soe and Hikae are exactly alike but the Shin is different. The Shin of variation No. 1 is tilted 10°—15° diagonally to the right rear.

In the basic upright arrangement the Shin and Soe both slant diagonally toward the left front but in variatian No. 1 the Shin and Soe are spread far apart which gives the composition a spacious look; therefore in order to make it easier to remember it is called "Open Variation No. 1".

Care should be taken not to put too many Jushi in this open space not to destroy the attractive sense of spaciousness which has been created.

— 46 —

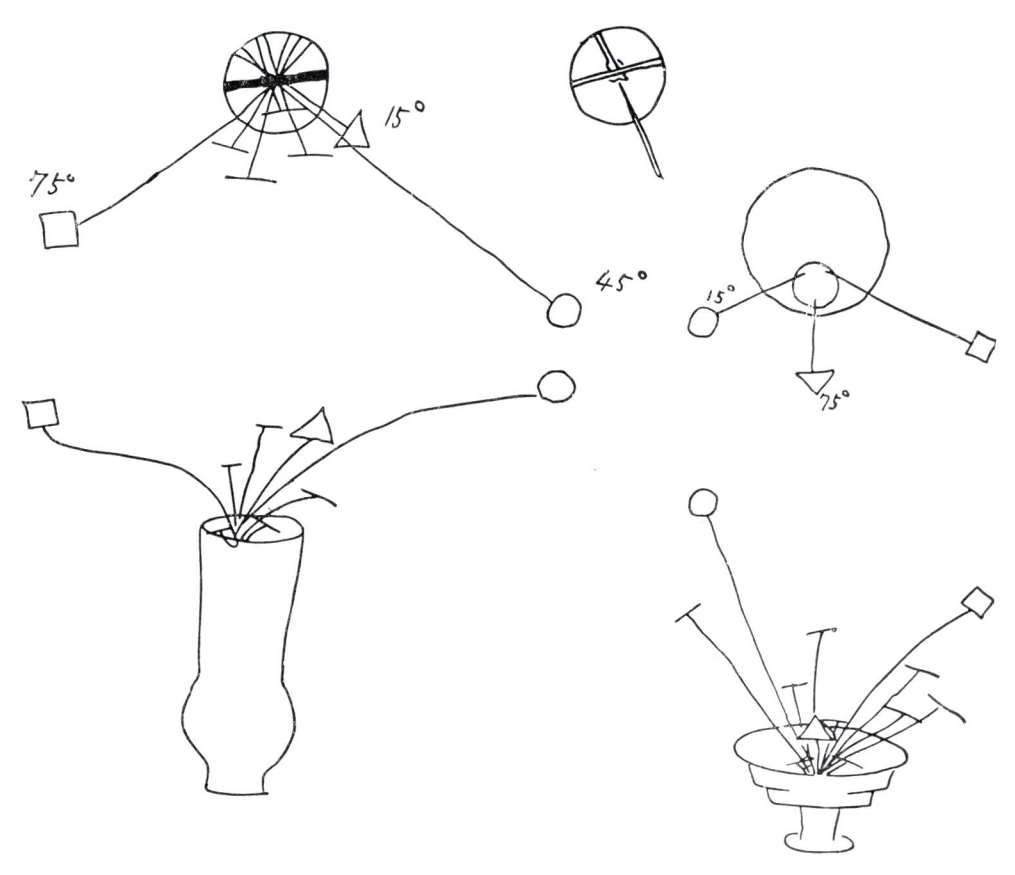

Variation No. 3 upright arrangement, Moribana

Material :——Poppies
Container :——Gray compote

Variation No. 3 is called "Flower with three-way front".

The Hikae is placed in front and the Shin and Soe open out like a fan. When selecting the material or the container, the fact should be taken into consideration that this style looks better in a Western style room than in a Japanese room.

The poppy used for the Shin is cut to its full length, which happened to be just one and one-half of the dish measurement, and exactly the standard measurement.

The length of the Soe is three-fourths of the Shin, and that of the Hikae three-fourths of the Soe. The Hikae in the photograph looks very short, but it is tilted 75° straight forward and so looks much shorter because it was photographed from the front. The very short flower seen in the back of the Hikae is the Jushi.

This form is suitable for most kinds of flowers, such as tulips, roses, lilies, chrysanthemums, irises, stocks or dahlias. These are very good flowers to use for practice.

Variation No. 3 slanting arrangement, Nageire

Material:—Carnations
Vase: —Black glass vase

This arrangement is very simple, only 5 carnations being used. No fixtures are needed.

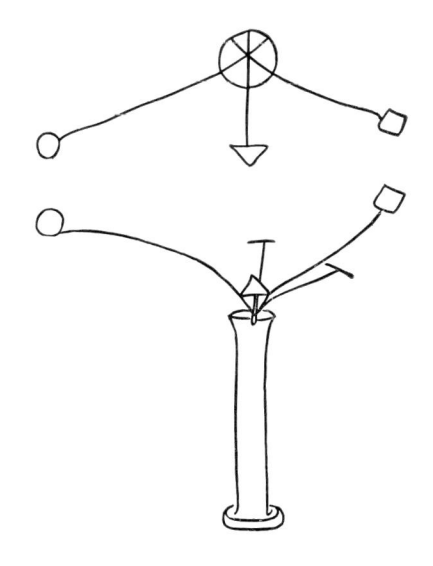

Variation No. 4 upright arrangement, Nageire

Materials: ——Wistaria branch and camellia
Vase: ——Yellow ceramic vase

The characteristic of Variation No. 4 is "Abbreviation of a main branch." As expressed in the sub-title, this arrangement consists of two main stems, the Shin and Hikae, the Soe being eliminated from the three main stems.

This form is especially suited for small pieces, as it is a simple and yet impressive style of arrangement.

First, place a long length of wistaria branch (Shin) in the vase, diagonally to the right front. Then a camellia (Hikae) is added on the opposite left side tilting 75° diagonally forward. Needless to say, this form can also be used for Moribana.

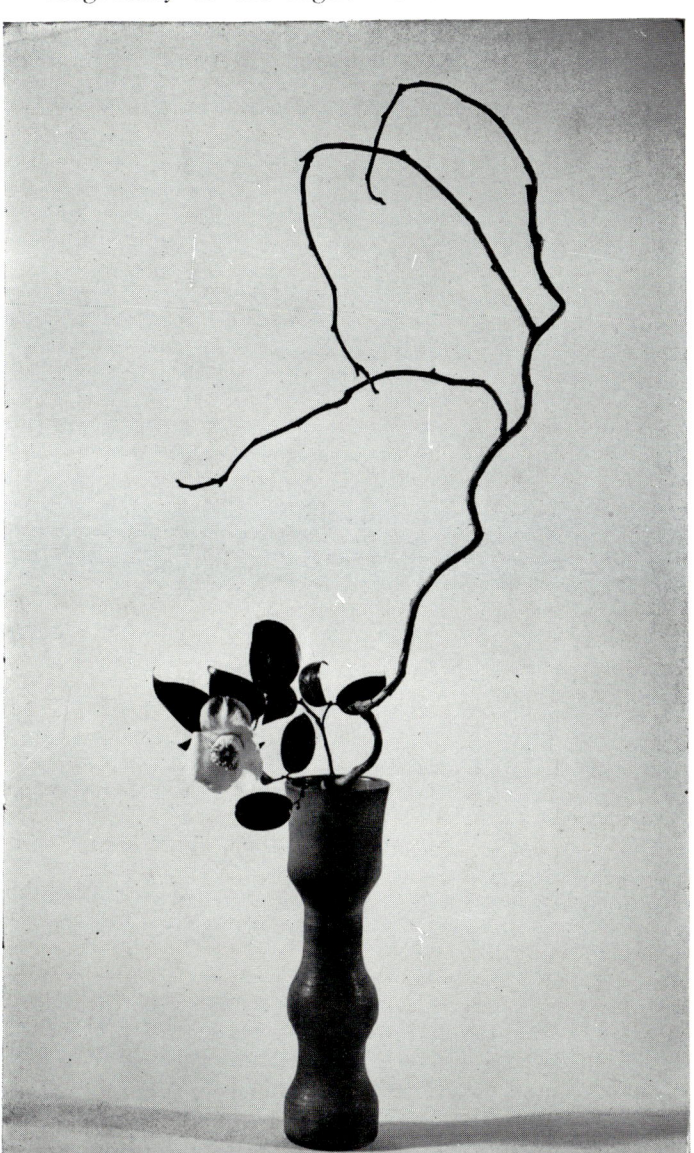

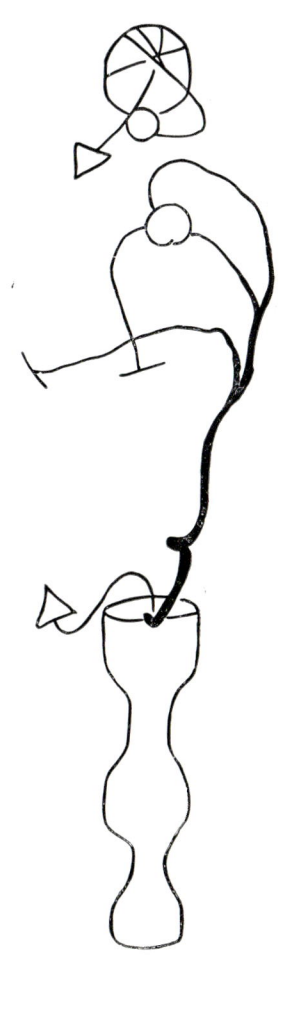

— 49 —

Variation No. 4
upright arrangement, Moribana

Materials :—
 Pussy-willow and tulip

Container :—
 Gray ceramic dish

Materials :—
 Holly and magnolia

Container :—
 Green and yellow glass compote

Variation No. 5 upright arrangement, Moribana

Materials :—— Ranunculus and anemone
Container :—— Shallow white porcelain dish

Variation No. 5 is called the divided style, or double arrangement. Normally, the flowers are arranged in one kenzan; but Variation No. 5 is arranged with one main stem, out of the three main stems, in one kenzan, and the other two in another kenzan, so that if the Shin and Hikae are in one kenzan, the Soe will be in the other kenzan, as shown in the photograph.

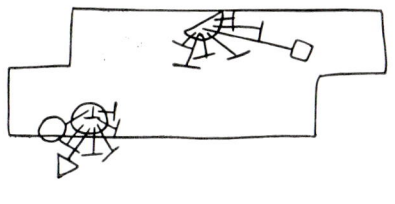

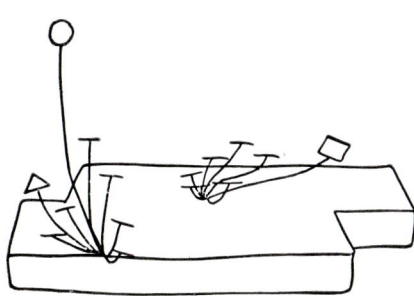

For this arrangement, ranunculus has been used for Shin, Soe and Hikae, and anemone for Jushi. This method of dividing one arrangement of flowers in two kenzans and placing them apart in one dish can be applied to the upright or slanting arrangement, and also for the variation styles; but the easiest way to learn the basic form is to practice the basic upright and slanting styles.

Variation No. 5 Moribana

Materials:—Japanese quince and cedar
Container:—Blue porcelain dish

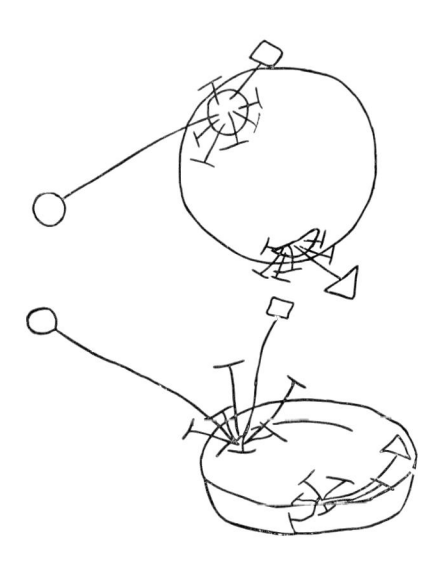

The photograph shows quince blossoms used as the three main branches, with the Shin and Soe in a round kenzan in the back and Hikae in front. The length of the Shin is for a small size arrangement, and the length of the Soe is three-fourths of the Shin, and the Hikae is three-fourths of the Soe. The style of arrangement is the same as that of Variation No. 1 slanting arrangement.

Hide the kenzan well with Jushi branches and leaves. The kenzan is very noticeable in this Variation No. 5 unless it is well covered with flowers or branches.

Variation No. 5

Example 1:

Material:—
Chrysanthemums (purple and white)

Container:—
Round porcelain dish

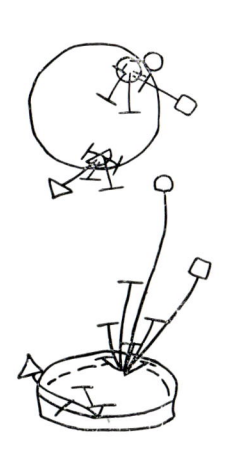

Example 2:

Materials:——Rhododendron and small white chrysanthemums

Container:——Pale blue porcelain dish

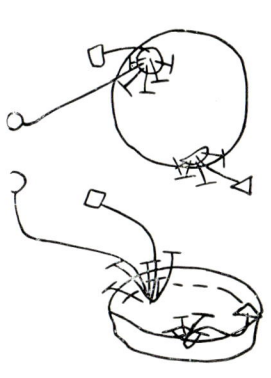

— 53 —

Basic Position of kenzan in Variation No. 5

Place the kenzan, one at left rear, and the other at front center. As shown in the photograph. It will not look well to place both of the kenzan in the front or in the rear of the container.

Example 3.

Variation No. 5 reminds one somewhat of a real scene; therefore, keep the length of Shin comparatively short as in small size arrangements, and arrange it compactly and neatly, but in a comparatively large dish so as to make the whole look larger.

A combination of branches and flowers is the best for this form of arrangement but it is also a very suitable form for flowers alone. If short flowers such as camellias, tulips, anemones, poppies, primroses, hyacinths, and daisies are used, this method of dividing an arrangement into two parts will help to emphasize the width of the composition.

This form is often used for water-plants in summer to help create a cool atmosphere.

Example 4.

Variation No. 5 always has space between the divided kenzans, and this space plays an important role in the arrangement of the flowers.

· Space made by lack of branches
· Space between the divided kenzans

Pay close attention to this space, for it will be noted that there is a great difference in having space in certain places.

The space in this arrangement is created by a void between the branches, and it is like the margin in paintings. The margin has a different strength from that of the painting itself, and the effectiveness of the margin is well realized in the case of paintings; but the space in the art of flower arrangement is usually much harder to realize, and often is passed by without notice. One can find great strength in a space, where there is no branch, and the Sogetsu School values this as very precious in the art of flower arrangement.

Variation No. 6 horizontal arrangement, Moribana

Material :——Rose
Container :——Small compote

Normally a flower piece has a background and is viewed from the front but when it is placed on a dining table or in the center of a reception room, or of an exhibition hall, it will be seen from all four sides.

The flowers arranged for this all-round view are called Variation No. 6. As shown in the photograph, the Shin is in almost the same horizontal line as the vase. This arrangement is therefore called horizontal arrangement.

Study the photograph and diagram and observe the stems in this arrangement spread in three directions.

Place the kenzan in the right side of the dish, and press the stem of the rose (Shin) straight down on the kenzan and then slant it almost to a horizontal line, about 85°—90°. Then take the Soe stem of the rose and slant it 60°—70° diagonally to the right front and tilt the Hikae rose straight back 75°. Placing the Hikae in this manner is entirely new here, and this will divide a circle in three, allowing the three main stems to branch out in three directions.

The two roses and a few leaves are placed around neatly, as shown in the diagram.

When the arrangement is completed this far, take care to hide the kenzan well with the small branches of roses and leaves, as this arrangement will be seen from all sides. It will be well to keep in mind that the special point of the Sogetsu School dining table flower style is to arrange it very low in the center.

In selecting a container for this arrangement, the size of the dining table must be taken into consideration.

Arranging an abundance of flowers in a small dish is very attractive. It is also a good idea to expose much water in summer to evoke a cool atmosphere.

75°

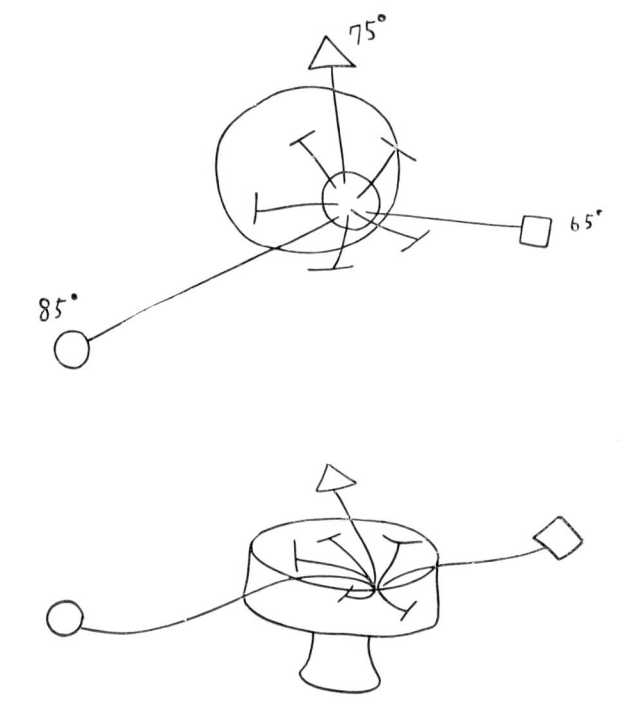

65°

85°

— 57 —

Variation No. 6
upright arrangement

Material:—
  Easter lily and daisy

Container:—
  Basket

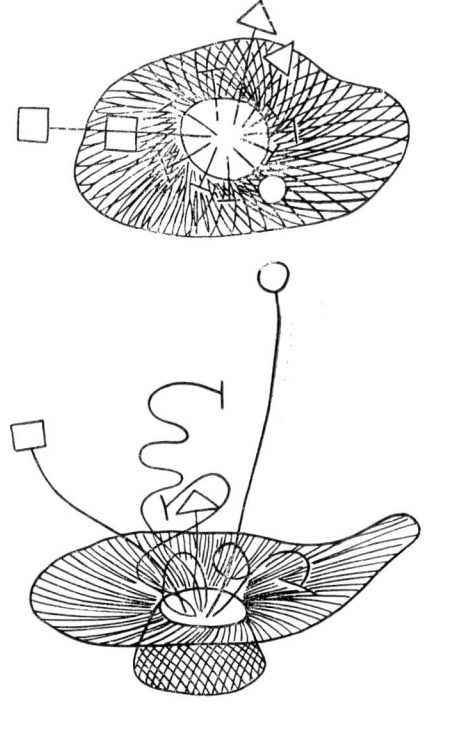

If the arrangement is to be seen from all four sides, for instance, in the center of a reception room, sales room, waiting room or in the center of an exhibition hall, it can be arranged in the upright arrangement and set on a high stool.

Variation No. 7

1. Floating arrangement
2. Spread flower (flat arrangement directly on table)
3. Morimono (platter design)

Variation No. 7 includes the above three styles.

Floating arrangement:

Materials:——Bitter-sweet and chrysanthemum
Container:——Red and black lacquer plate

As seen in the picture, fill the plate with water and lay a long spray of bitter-sweet in it with the tip flowing out of the plate, and float white chrysanthemums on the plates.

There is a beauty of direct closeness in the combination of flowers and water in these floating arrangements. The purpose of the arrangement is not only to see the flowers, but at the same time to enjoy the surface of the water, which adds a delightful sensation of coolness. This arrangement is a little different from that of the ordinary Moribana.

Floating arrangement:

Materials:——Water lily and asparagus
Container:——White frothy glass plate

This arrangement harmonizes well with Western style surroundings, whether on a dining table or on the guest room table; but this arrangement calls for special care in the harmony of flowers and dish. Large flowers will offer more interesting and striking variations than flowers too small in size, and it is best to experiment with this type of arrangement freely, with little regard to the rules.

No kenzan is used with this arrangement, but if it is necessary to use one make every effort to conceal the kenzan completely.

Spread flower: Example 1.

Materials:——Flowering quince and chrysanthemums

Spread flower means to lay flowers directly on a table, and if it is done with thought as to the color and shape, many variations can be obtained as when pictures are drawn with ease.

For example, this photograph shows sprigs of flowering quince laid on the table for a base, with flowers laid on top like patterns.

Here, the small flowering twigs are laid amongst the branches.

The spread flower is done impromptu, and it is only for a short while. It is therefore, not necessary to make it last or give the flowers water.

This arrangement also harmonizes well with Western style surroundings, especially for the dining table and will be in much demand in the future, so it is well worth practicing with varied materials.

Spread flower : Example 2.
Materials : ——Sankirai (smilax china) and red dahlia

Variation No. 7: Morimono (Platter design)

Materials:——Apples and white camellia
Container:——Black lacquer tray

For this type of arrangement, vegetables or fruit can be used with an appropriate sized Rhodea Japonica (or other short plant with roots) or an orchid with the roots washed off, or small branches of pine or plum blossoms.

In this arrangement, ingenuity is needed for the color scheme, and also harmony in combining large and small size or round and oblong shaped objects, is very important.

Do not just pile the fruit or vegetables into a basket or on platters, but utilize to advantage the beautiful colors and the varied shapes they have, and arrange them artistically and freely, studying them as you do with a flower arrangement to make daily living much happier and more interesting.

The example in this picture is very simple and easy enough for anyone to follow, but it is filled with the beauty of simplicity.

On a black lacquer tray two apples are laid for Shin and Soe, one of them on its side, and a white camellia for Hikae, and thus it is completed. It makes a clear-colored, neat and smart decoration for the Tokonoma (alcove) or to put on a table.

Suitable containers to use for these arrangements are a platter, bowl, shallow dish or large leaves, such as banana or palm leaves and even a bamboo mat or small board or tray, or anything else besides these already mentioned, if they are simple and without decoration.

Baskets are quite handy and have their own unique quality.

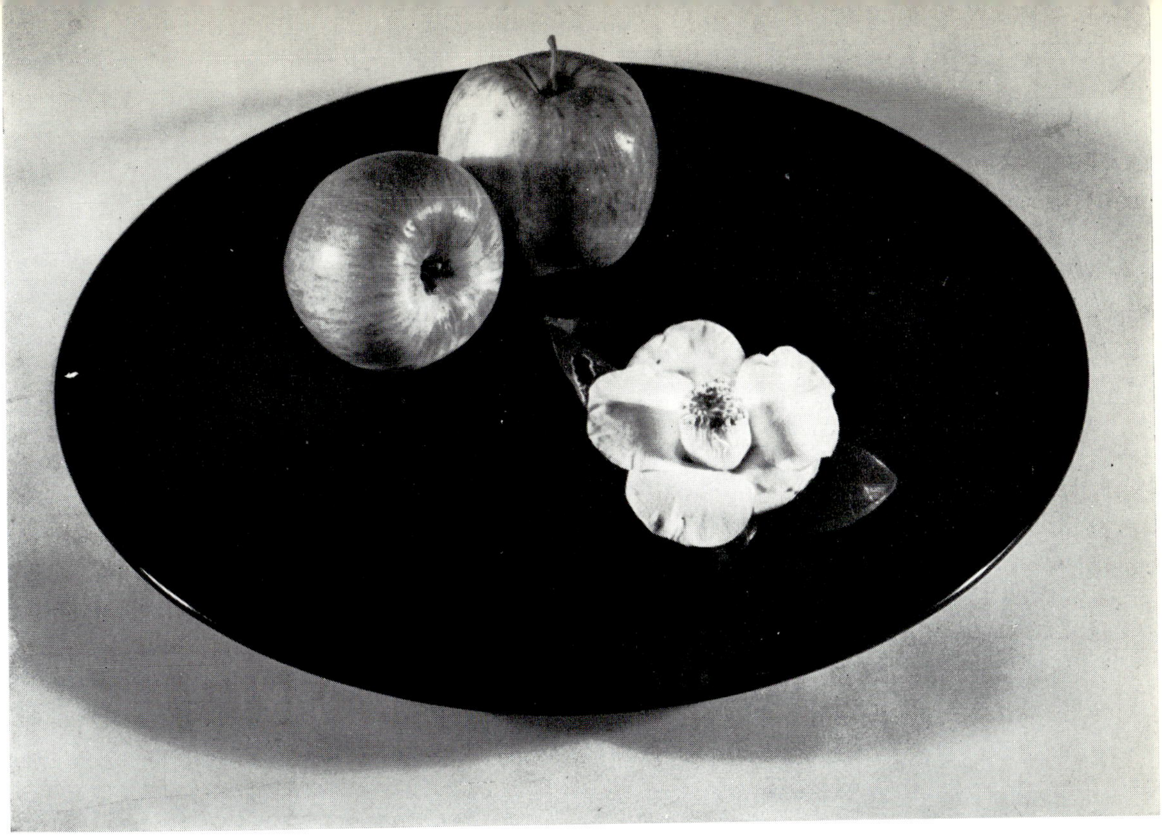

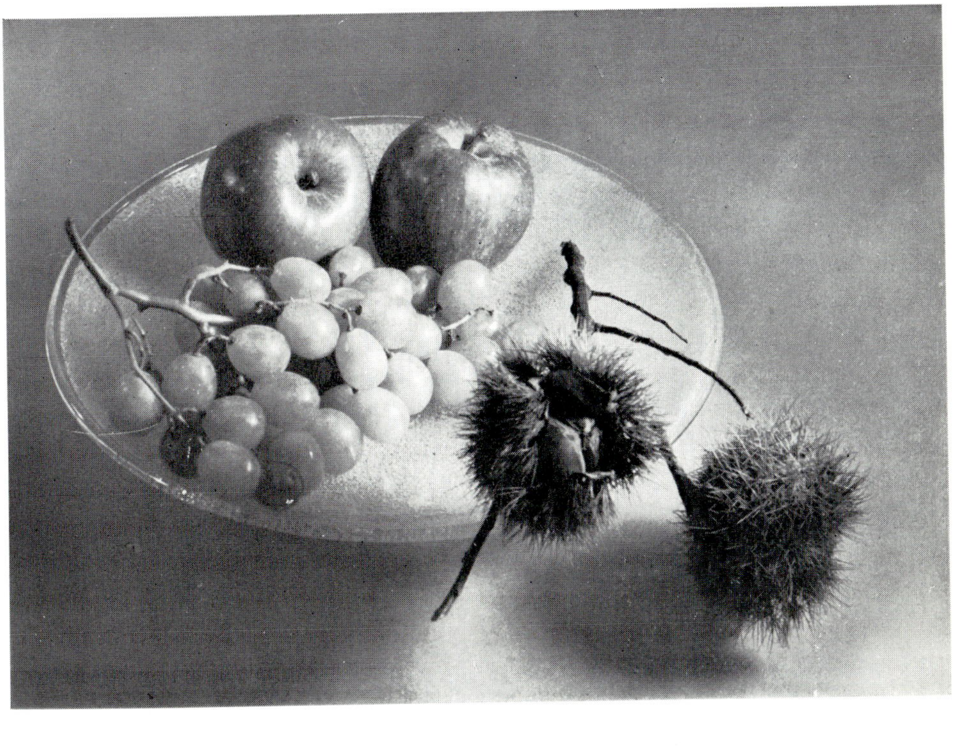

Variation No. 8 Combination Arrangement

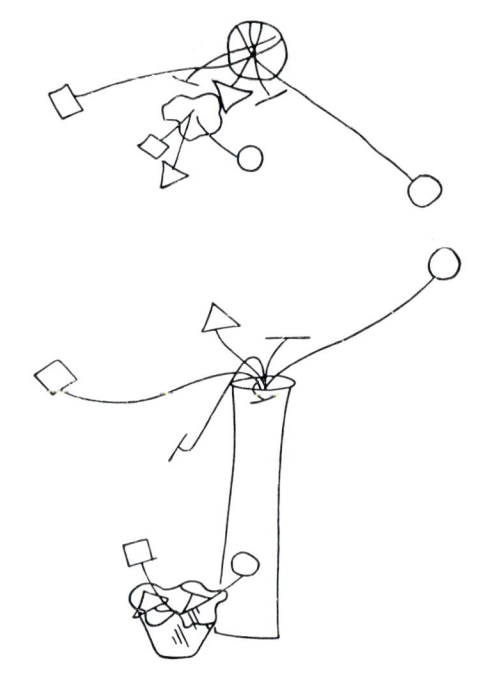

Materials: — Mimosa-acacia and sweetpeas with leaves

Container: — Tall glass vase and glass bowl

Variation No. 8 is also called combination arrangement. Two containers are combined for this flower arrangement.

At times two similar containers are used together, or two separate forms of flowers are arranged each in a different kenzan and placed in a large shallow dish to create a blended look of wholeness.

In the first photograph, the Moribana and Nageire are combined, but the containers are of the same material, with the Nageire vase made of wistaria colored glass with dark blue lines running through it, and the small bowl made of white frothy glass. When two containers are combined, the color combination is the most important factor.

For the Nageire composition the acacia is arranged in Variation No. 3 hanging arrangement. For the small dish at the foot, only the Hikae is put in, and it brings out the sweet brightness of spring.

Note that the Shin is in an altogether different direction from any form introduced so far. This form with its Shin drooping down, is called the hanging arrangement. But, of course, depending on the shapes of the branches used, this can be arranged in upright or slanting arrangements.

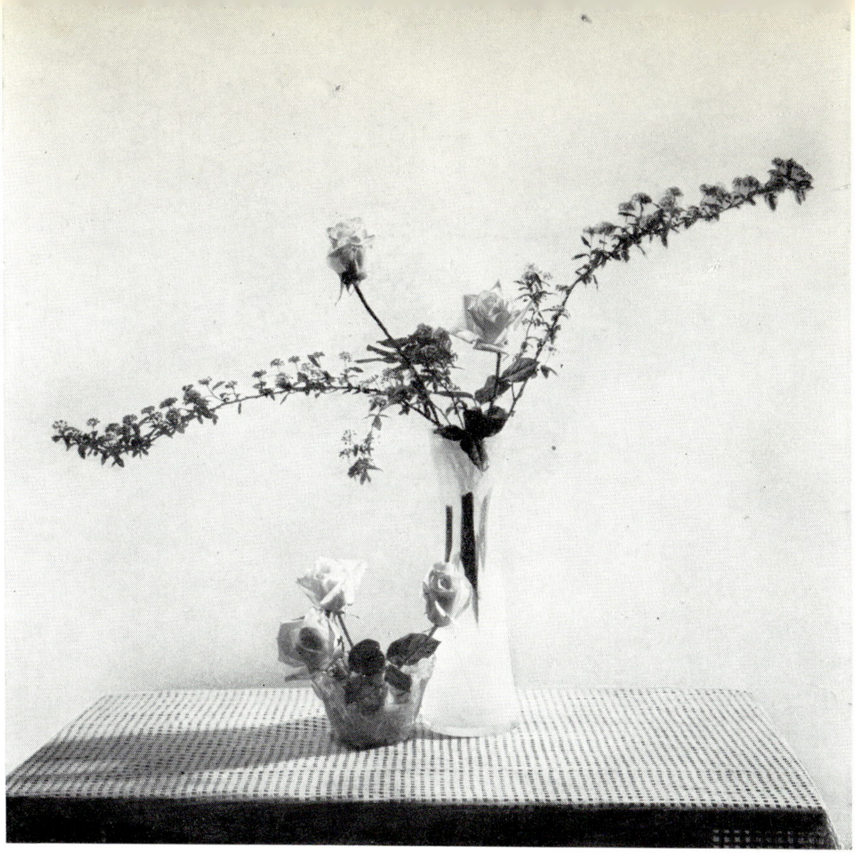

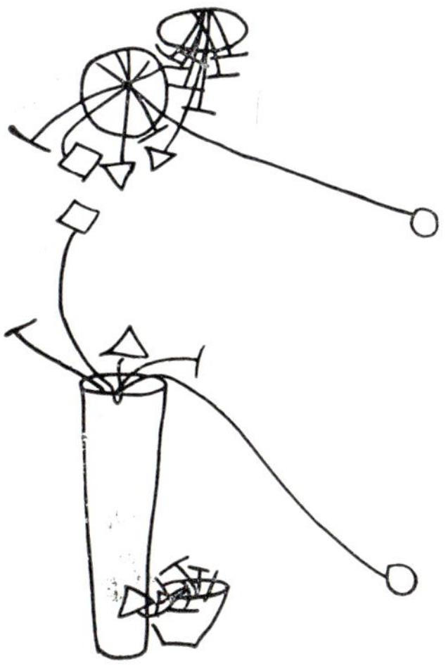

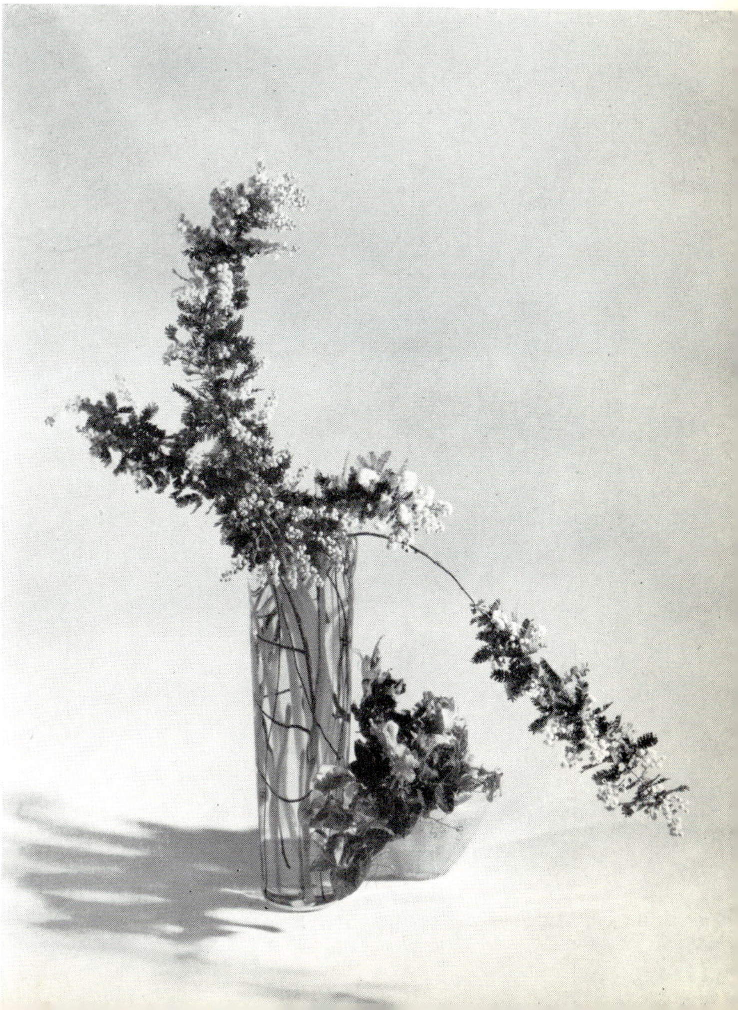

Instructions on all the Basic and Variation Styles of the Sogetsu School have been given in this book.

After earnest study and intensive practice of these styles, one will be able to master the technique and create fine examples of one's own.

The Sogetsu School encourages the practice of free style, or individual expression in the art of flower arranging, but only after much practice in the basic or fundamental forms.

As can be seen in the following pages, poetic license may be taken to express individual thoughts and feelings, but at the same time a sense of color-blending, conformity of design with material and container, as has been taught in the foregoing chapters on basic styles, must always be kept in mind.

Materials:——Mustard seeds, gladiolus
Container:——White porcelain vase

Materials:——Hawthorn and easter lily
Container:——Black glazed dish

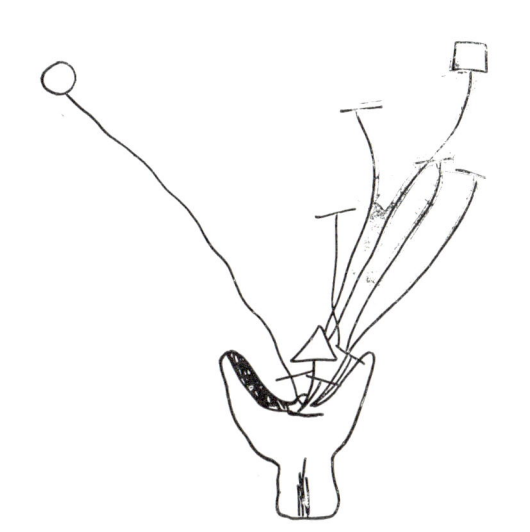

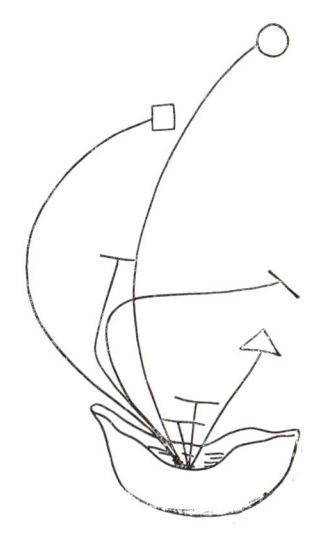

Materials:—Bamboo leaves, pine and carnation

Container:—Black lacquer with gold pattern

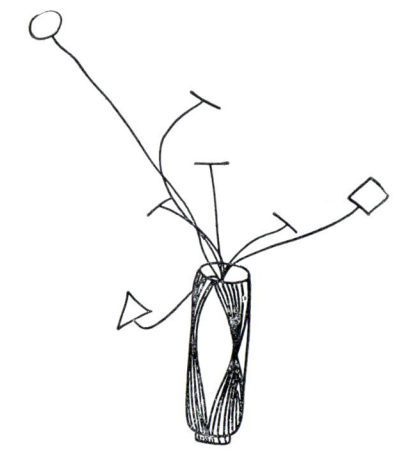

— 68 —

Materials: — Snow-willow and yellow lily

Container: — Bon-bon dish

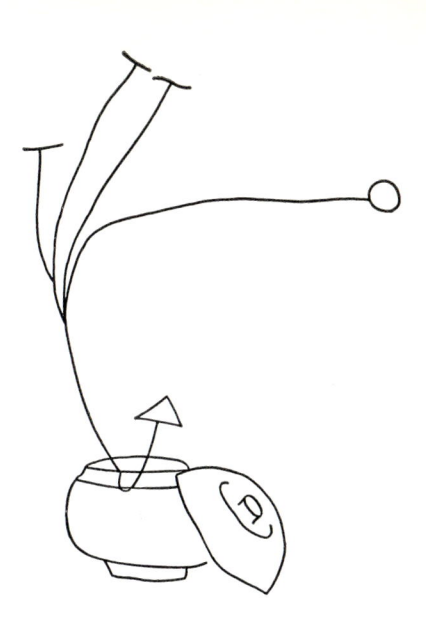

Material: — White camellia
Vase: — Gray ceramic vase

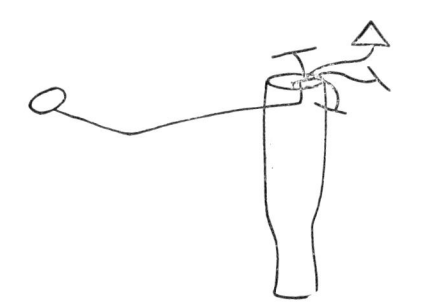

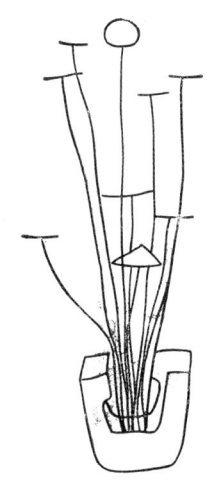

Material: — Narcissus
Container: — Black ceramic vase

Material:—

    Camellia

Container:—

    White bamboo basket

Materials:—Rose and bamboo leaves

Container:—

    Brown basket

Materials: —— Blue and pink hydrangea and bulrushes
Container: —— Smoky glass container

Materials: ——
Yellow Tulip
and White Vine

Container: ——
Black compote

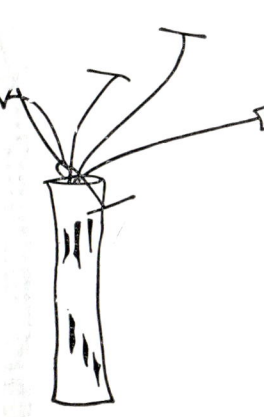

Materials: —— Mauve heather and pale pink roses
Container: —— White frothy glass vase

Material: —Purple clematis
Vase: —Pale gray ceramic vase

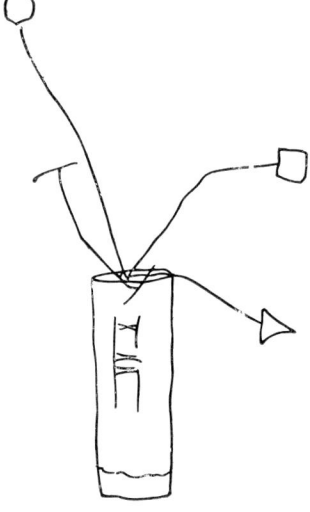

— 74 —

Materials: —— Bitter-sweet and anthurium

Vase: —— White and gray ceramic vase

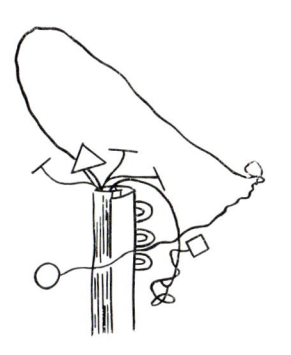

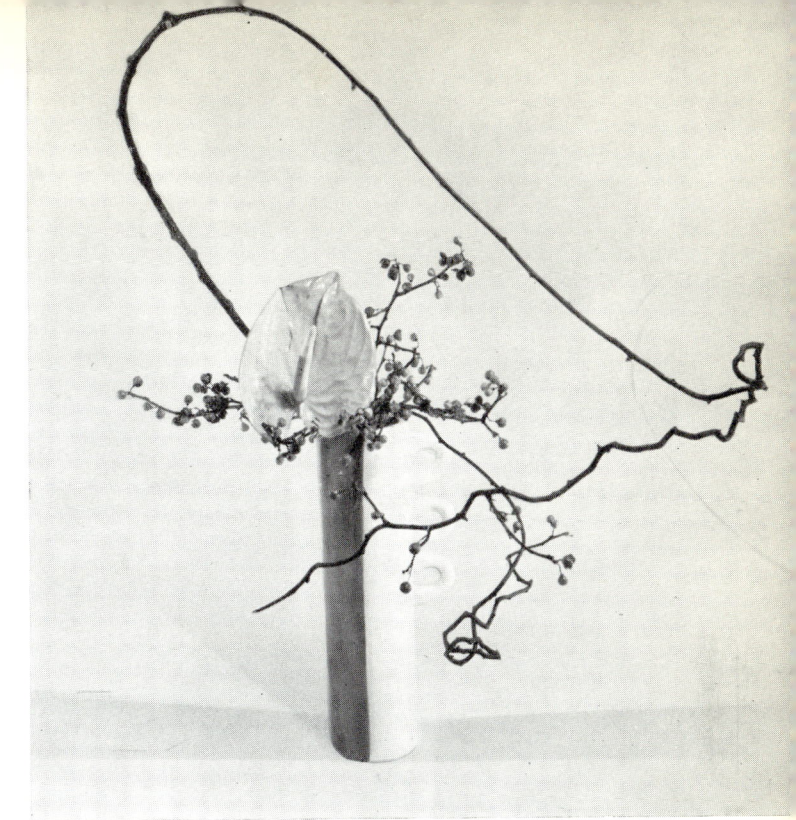

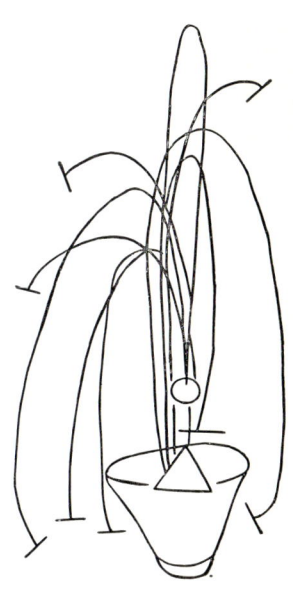

Materials: —— Pampus-leaves, water lily

Container: —— Smoky glass

Materials:—White pampus grass, black driftwood and pink water lilies
Container:—White porcelain dish

Materials:—Pine and camellia
Container:—Large sea-shell

Materials:——Anthurium and orchid
Container:——Brown ceramic vase

Materials:——Yellow tulips and asparagus
Container:——Basket

Materials :—Honey-suckle and rose
Container :—Ceramic vase

Materials :—Bulrush, yellow water lily
Container :—White basket

Materials :——Anthurium and orchid
Container :——Brown ceramic vase

Materials :——Yellow tulips and asparagus
Container :——Basket

Materials :—Honey-suckle and rose
Container :—Ceramic vase

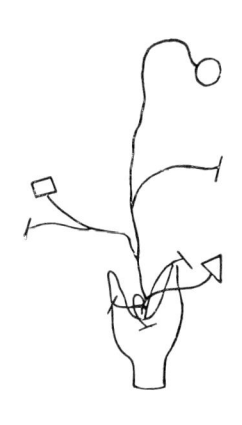

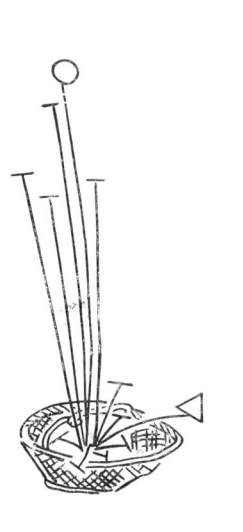

Materials :—Bulrush, yellow water lily
Container :—White basket

Materials:—Sweetpeas, camellia leaves and dried material
Container:—Yellow lacquer dish